D0017878

YUSEI MATSUI
1
TIME FOR ASSASSINATION

ASSASSINATION CLASSROOM 1 CONTENTS

(ANSWER SHEET)

CLASS 1	Killing Time in Homeroom	= 005
CLASS 2	No Time to Strike Out	= 057
CLASS 3	The Perfect Time to Help Out	× 081
CLASS 4	Time to Get Down to Work	= 101
CLASS 5	Making Time for Karma	÷ 121
CLASS 6	It's Time to Make a Choice	= 143
CLASS 7	Time for a Refreshing Drink	< 163
RECESS	Koro Sensei's Drawing Song	= 182

rade	3	Class	E	Name	CONTENTS	Score	

SHFF
3-E
CLASS 1 | KILLING TIME IN HOMEROOM
FLOOP
LUB-DUB
FLOOP
FLOOP
LUB-DUB
LUB-DUB
LET'S GET GOING!
EVERYONE STAND FOR THE PLEDGE!
Attendance
FLOOP
UM...
UH...

KLACK
KLACK
NOW!!
KLACK
EECH

Class 1 Killing Time in Homeroom

START!!

GET READY!!
KLCK
KLACK
GRIN
...ASSAS-SINS.
WE ARE...
gulp.
FI-I-I-RE!!!!
POW POW POW POW POW POW

SO I GUESS WE'RE NOT DOING THE PLEDGE THEN...
POW
POW
POW POW
POW

I'M SORRY, I CAN'T HEAR YOU OVER ALL THESE GUNSHOTS. COULD YOU SPEAK UP, PLEASE?
UM ...
HERE!!
POW POW POW POW
OKANO.
HERE !!
KATA-OKA.
HERE !!

OKAY. YOU MAY KEEP SHOOTING WHILE I TAKE ATTENDANCE.
ISOGAI.
HUH?
POW
POW POW

ZLIP
WONDERFUL! I'M SO HAPPY!
EVERY-ONE'S HERE... AND ON TIME!
ALL THOSE BULLETS... AND WE MISSED?!
HE'S TOO FAST !!
DINK
WE'RE ASSAS-SINS. AND OUR TARGET IS...
...OUR TEACHER.
DINK
DINK

YOU HAVE TO COME UP WITH A MORE ORIGINAL PLAN.
I'M TOO QUICK FOR YOU.
I CAN MOVE AT MACH 20, REMEMBER?

MAYBE WE'RE HITTING YOU, BUT YOU'RE JUST PRETENDING WE DIDN'T!
YEAH! YOU'RE CHEATING!
BOO! BOO!
...

ARE YOU REALLY DODGING ALL THOSE BULLETS?
WELL, THEY'RE MORE LIKE BB'S THAN BULLETS...

...THESE BULLETS— BB'S—ARE HARMLESS TO YOU...
LIKE I SAID...
KCHIK

OKAY. SOMEONE PLEASE HAND ME A GUN THAT'S LOADED.

SP
BLAM
LORCH
BUT THEY WERE DESIGNED ESPECIALLY FOR ME.
SQUIGGL SQUIGGL SQUIGGL

SO PLEASE DON'T USE THE GUN INSIDE THE CLASSROOM UNLESS YOU ARE TRYING TO KILL ME.
BUT I WOULDN'T WANT ANYBODY TO ACCIDENTALLY SHOOT THEIR EYE OUT WITH THESE.

HEH.
OF COURSE, I CAN REGENERATE LOST LIMBS AND SUCH IN A FEW SECONDS.
THEY CAN CUT THROUGH ME LIKE PUDDING.
ZL
ORP

WOM
WOM
I HOPE YOU CAN KILL ME...
...BEFORE GRADUATION.
RING
RING
RING
RING
NOW PLEASE PUT AWAY YOUR GUNS, PICK UP ALL THE BULLETS, AND LET'S GET THIS ROOM IN ORDER.
IT'S TIME TO START CLASS.
KUNUGIGAOKA JUNIOR HIGH, CLASS 3-E IS THE ASSASSINATION CLASSROOM.
IT'S WEIRD, BUT WE'VE KINDA GOTTEN USED TO IT.

...
THE BLUE ONE?
COR-RECT!!
THE "WHO" IN THIS SENTENCE BEGINS THE RELATIVE CLAUSE.
He said "who is the
I have a friend who
Who wants to eat
Who left this sucker on
Gamma
WHICH OF MY TENTACLES IS POINTING TO THE SENTENCE WITH THE RELATIVE CLAUSE?
OKAY... KIMURA...
SO...HOW DID WE END UP IN THIS SITUATION?
HEY...
...NA-GISA!
IT'S NOON...
...AND YOU CAN STILL SEE THE CRESCENT MOON.
TWO THINGS HAP-PENED...
...AT THE START OF OUR THIRD YEAR.

THE MOON !!
SEVENTY PERCENT OF THE MOON IS JUST... GONE!! IT'LL NEVER BE FULL AGAIN!!
WHAT HAPPENED TO THE MOON?!
AND NEXT YEAR AT THIS TIME I'M GOING TO DO THE SAME THING TO YOUR PLANET EARTH.
I'M THE ONE WHO DISINTEGRATED PART OF THE MOON.
NICE TO MEET YOU.
ALSO, I'M YOUR NEW TEACHER. I HOPE WE GET ALONG WELL.

AS IF THAT WASN'T STRANGE ENOUGH...
...THEN IT GOT WEIRD!

MY NAME'S KARASUMA. I'M FROM THE MINISTRY OF DEFENSE.
WHAT I'M ABOUT TO TELL YOU...
...IS EXTREMELY CONFIDENTIAL. THIS IS A TOP SECRET OPERATION, AND I NEED YOUR HELP.

TO PUT IT BLUNTLY ...
...I WANT YOU TO KILL THIS MONSTER!!

FSSST
HOW RUDE!
I WAS BORN AND RAISED ON EARTH!
UM...
EX-CUSE ME...
IS THIS GUY SOME KIND OF, UH, ALIEN WHO'S COME TO, LIKE, DESTROY THE PLANET?
ONLY THE WORLD LEADERS KNOW OF THIS.
...BEFORE THE WORLD FINDS OUT, CAUSING A MASS PANIC.
SO WE'RE TRYING TO KILL HIM...
ZLIP
IN OTHER WORDS, YOUR ASSIGN-MENT IS TO...
BUT HE'S TELLING YOU THE TRUTH.
SORRY, THAT INFORMA-TION IS CLASSIFIED.
...AND HE PLANS TO DESTROY THE EARTH NEXT YEAR AFTER YOUR GRADUATION.
ALSO, HE DESTROYED MOST OF THE MOON...

SWISH
SW
ISH
...ASSAS-SINATE YOUR TEACHER.
AS YOU CAN SEE ...
SWISH
PLUK
PLUK
SWISH
...HE'S INCREDIBLY FAST!!
RIGHT NOW HE'S TRIMMING MY EYEBROWS WITH AMAZING ACCURACY AND SKILL!
SWISH
IN OTHER WORDS ...
...IF HE REALLY TRIED TO ESCAPE US...
HE'S POWERFUL ENOUGH TO BLOW UP THE MOON...
...AND TO FLY AT MACH 20!!
...WE'D NEVER BE ABLE TO CATCH HIM—UNTIL IT WAS TOO LATE!

SO I MADE A PROPOSAL TO THE WORLD LEADERS.
SNAP
BUT THAT WOULD BE...
...BO-RING.
ALTHOUGH I HAVE NO INTENTION OF GETTING KILLED...
TAP TAP
...I WANT TO BE THE TEACHER OF CLASS 3-E AT KUNUGIGAOKA JUNIOR HIGH.
WHY?!
WE... DON'T KNOW.
BUT WE ACCEPTED HIS OFFER...
...UNDER THE CONDITION THAT HE NEVER HARM ANY STUDENTS.
AT LEAST WHILE HE'S TEACH-ING...
...WE'LL BE ABLE TO KEEP AN EYE ON HIM.

...THIRTY OF YOU...
AND BEST OF ALL...
...CAN ATTEMPT TO KILL HIM EVERY DAY AT CLOSE RANGE!!
BL
AM
FSSST
DIDN'T I TELL YOU THAT YOU MAY ONLY TRY TO KILL ME AS LONG AS IT DOESN'T INTERFERE WITH YOUR STUDIES?
GO STAND IN THE CORNER.
SOR-RY...
LIGH. I HATE HOW RED HIS FACE GETS WHEN HE'S MAD.
KRCK
NAKA-MURA...
WHY DO WE HAVE TO ASSAS-SINATE HIM?!
AND WHAT'S IN IT FOR US?
WHY DID THIS THING WANT TO BE OUR TEACHER?
IT WAS SURREAL.

¥?!
Ten b-b-b...
BELIEVE ME WHEN I SAY ASSASSINATING HIM WILL SAVE THE WORLD!
IF YOU KILL HIM!
TEN BILLION IN COLD CASH!!

NEAT! HE'S LIKE A CHAMEL-EON!
SEE THOSE GREEN STRIPES? HE DOESN'T THINK YOU CAN DO IT.
LOOK.
GRIN
LUCKILY FOR YOU, HE DOESN'T CONSIDER YOU CHILDREN A THREAT.

SQUEEGEE SQUEEGEE
WHEN I WAS ATTACKED BY A STATE-OF-THE-ART FIGHTER PLANE...
WHY DID YOU POLISH IT FOR THEM?!
...I WAXED IT IN MIDAIR FOR THEM.
OF COURSE I DON'T.
YOU'RE NOT AN ARMY.

EXACTLY.
...I WANT ALL OF YOU TO LIVE THE REMAINING YEAR OF YOUR LIFE AS PRODUCTIVELY AS POSSIBLE!
SO UNTIL THEN...
JUST STRIKE WHILE HIS GUARD IS DOWN.
WE'LL GIVE YOU SPECIAL WEAPONRY—HARMLESS TO YOU, FATAL TO HIM!
BUT REMEMBER, THIS IS TOP SECRET. YOU MUST TELL NO ONE!
WE DON'T HAVE A LOT OF TIME.
AND NOWHERE TO GO IF HE DESTROYS THE EARTH.
RING
RING
RING
RING

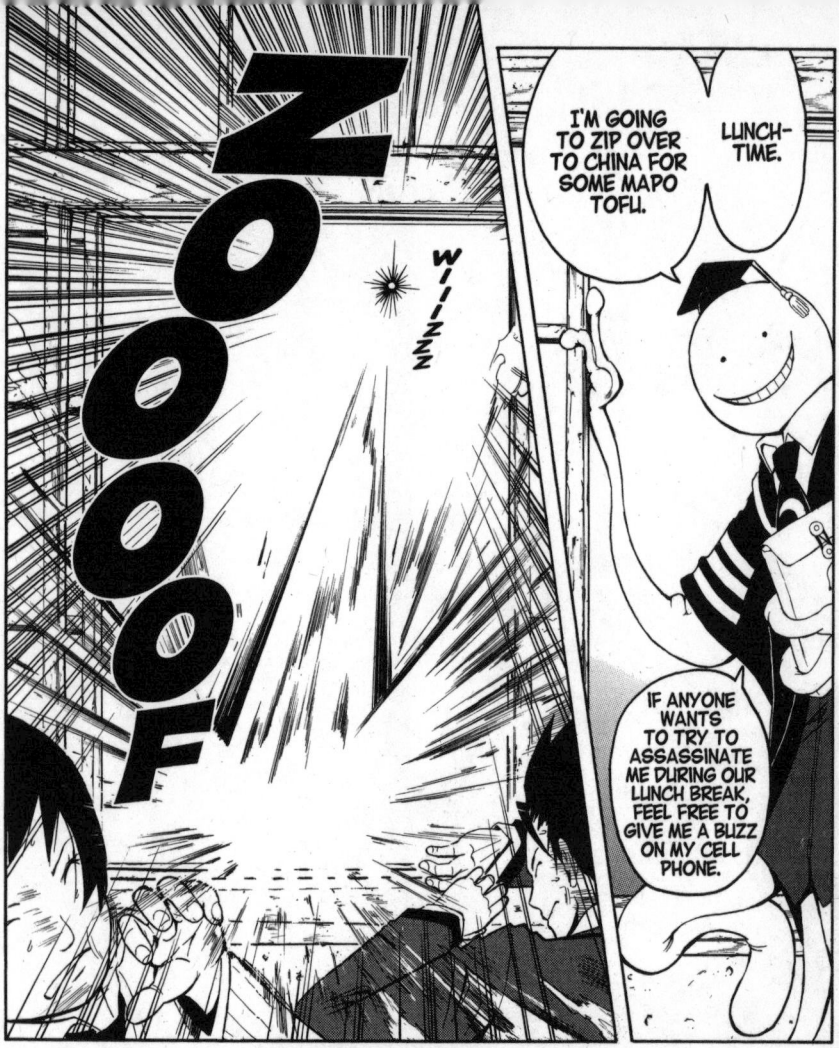
ZOOOOOOF
W-I-I-ZZZZ
I'M GOING TO ZIP OVER TO CHINA FOR SOME MAPO TOFU.
LUNCH-TIME.
IF ANYONE WANTS TO TRY TO ASSASSINATE ME DURING OUR LUNCH BREAK, FEEL FREE TO GIVE ME A BUZZ ON MY CELL PHONE.

NO WONDER THEY CAN'T SHOOT HIM DOWN WITH A MISSILE.
AT THAT SPEED, IT'S ABOUT A TEN-MINUTE FLIGHT TO SICHUAN PROVINCE TO GET AUTHENTIC MAPO TOFU.
MUST BE NICE TO BE ABLE TO FLY AT MACH 20...

SCRTCH SCRTCH
WHADDYA KNOW... THAT CRAZY FREAK IS GRADING OUR TESTS WHILE FLYING.
SERI-OUSLY ?!
YEAH.
HE LIKED MY ANSWER. HE EVEN DREW A LITTLE OCTOPUS NEXT TO IT.
Perfect!
BUT WE'RE STILL CLASS E.
YOU KNOW, HE'S NOT A BAD TEACHER...
YEAH.
I TRIED TO ASSASSIN-ATE HIM AFTER SCHOOL BUT HE STARTED TUTOR-ING ME IN MATH...
AND I ACED THE TEST!
WELL...
YEAH...
SO WHY WORK SO HARD FOR NOTHING?
EXACTLY.
NEW HOLLOW ENGLISH

WELL...
...THE STUDENTS OF CLASS E...
...ARE A LITTLE DIFFERENT ACTUALLY...

...SOME WEIRD SUPER-OCTOPUS THING...
WE HAVE TO ASSAS-SINATE...
...THAT FOR SOME REASON IS OUR TEACHER.
Chemistry
Art

HEY, NAGISA ...
TNK

KIND OF LIKE US...
WE MAY BE PART-TIME ASSASSINS, BUT WE'RE STILL FULL-TIME STUDENTS.

LET'S GO OVER THE PLAN.
C'MERE.

...
OKAY.

WE ALREADY KNOW WHEN HIS FACE HAS GREEN STRIPES, HE'S NOT TAKING US SERIOUSLY.
SORT OF...

YOU DO YOUR HOMEWORK LIKE I ASKED?
YOU FIGURE OUT WHAT IT MEANS WHEN HIS FACE CHANGES COLOR?

THE INTERESTING COLOR IS AFTER LUNCH. THAT'S WHEN IT TURNS—
I DON'T NEED TO KNOW—*YOU* DO.
AND BRIGHT RED WHEN A STUDENT GETS THE RIGHT ANSWER.
+1+1+1
+1+1x0+1
+1+1+1+1
=10
WHEN A STUDENT MAKES A MISTAKE, HIS FACE TURNS DARK PURPLE.
+1+1+1
+1+1x0+1
+1+1+1+1
=5

MY PLAN IS SIMPLE.
YOU STAB HIM...
...WHEN HIS GUARD IS DOWN.
ME...?
B-BUT...
B...

OH, COME ON...
GLARE
WE'RE CLASS E, REMEMBER?

THE SCHOOL'S LOSERS AND REJECTS.

THE "END CLASS."

STUCK IN SOME OLD CLASSROOM YOU HAVE TO CLIMB A MOUNTAIN TO GET TO.

...AND TREATED LIKE CRAP BY EVERYONE—INCLUDING THE TEACHERS!

ANY WAY...
...WE CAN.

DON'T LET ME DOWN, NAGISA!
...
HA HAHA HAHA ...

NAGISA'S BEING SENT TO CLASS E.
Class Transfer Notice
Shiota Nagisa
Because your academic achievement does not meet the standards of this school, you are hereby transferred to the
WHOA.
HE'S DONE FOR.
TIME TO UNFRIEND HIM...
I DON'T WANT OTHER PEOPLE TO THINK I KNOW HIM.
旧校舎 1km
本校舎 徒歩30m

WEL-COME BACK...
A SOU-VENIR.
WHAT'S WITH THE MISSILE ?
THE NAVY WAS WAITING FOR ME IN THE SEA OF JAPAN.

WHOA !!
ZWOOP

!

NAH.
TINK
IT MUST BE TOUGH BEING EVERY-ONE'S TARGET.
WOW ...

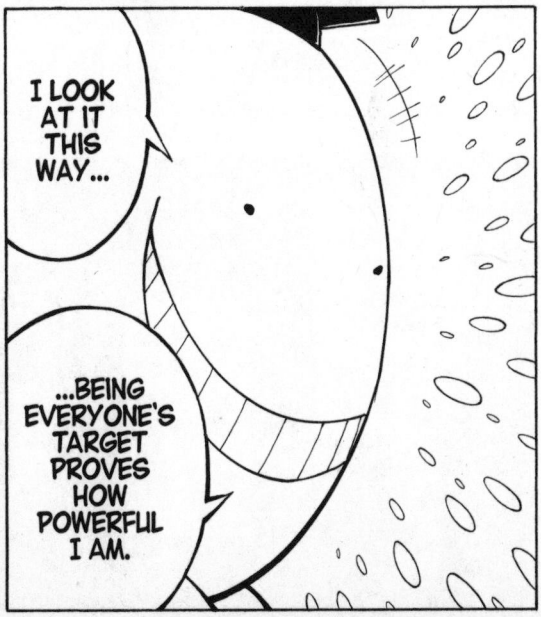
I LOOK AT IT THIS WAY...
...BEING EVERYONE'S TARGET PROVES HOW POWERFUL I AM.

NOW THEN ...
IT'S TIME FOR FIFTH PERIOD.
LIM ...
YEAH ...

AT LEAST...
...PEOPLE RECOGNIZE HIS POWER.

HE...
...DOESN'T LINDER-STAND.

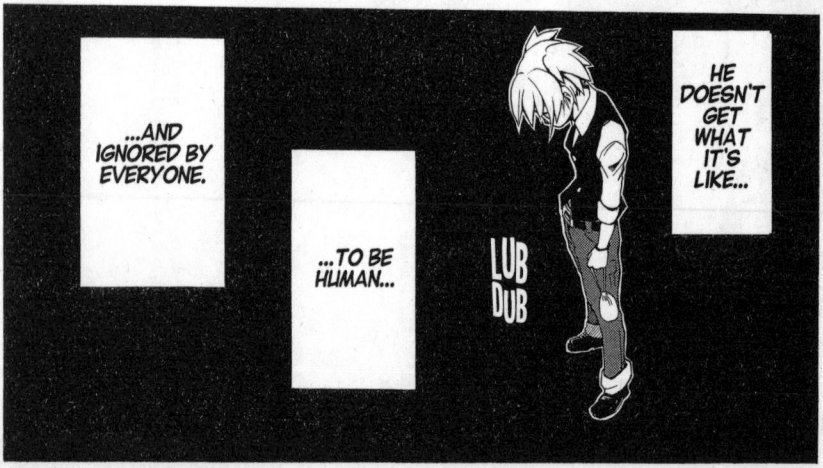
HE DOESN'T GET WHAT IT'S LIKE...
LUB DUB
...TO BE HUMAN...
...AND IGNORED BY EVERYONE.

I MIGHT ACTUALLY BE ABLE TO KILL HIM.
TING
TING
TING
YOU DESTROYED MY REPUTATION, YOU KNOW.
LUB DUB
AT LEAST NOW...
LUB DUB
...I WON'T HAVE TO SEE YOU ANYMORE.
LUB DUB
LUB
DUB
AFTER ALL...
...HE'LL IGNORE ME TOO— UNTIL IT'S TOO LATE.

PLEASE BRING THEM TO ME WHEN YOU'RE DONE.
I'LL BE CHECKING GRAMMAR AS WELL AS YOUR USE OF METAPHORS AND SIMILES.
The flower petals fell like colored snow. The vines writhed up from the ground like tentacles.

LET'S WRITE SOME FREE-VERSE POETRY.
Assention/Past
Auxiliary Verb
Collocation
Were
I'D LIKE YOU TO END ALL YOUR POEMS WITH THE WORD "TENTACLES."

IF YOU'RE DONE, YOU MAY LEAVE FOR THE DAY.
Oh, I get that reference!
"N-T... There's a big differ-ence."

I HAVE A QUESTION.
HM ...?
WHAT IS IT, KAYANO?
I KNOW THE SCHOOL YEAR HAS ALREADY STARTED, BUT...
...WHAT'S YOUR NAME?
WE CAN'T REALLY CALL OUR TEACHER "STRANGE OCTOPUS-THING WE HAVE TO KILL."
THAT'S A BIT LONG, YES...
YOU KNOW... I DON'T HAVE A NAME!
WHY DON'T YOU THINK OF ONE FOR ME?
BUT AFTER YOU FINISH YOUR POEM.
OKAY.
PSSSSSF

AH.
DONE ALREADY, NAGISA?
KLTTR
GRIN
FWIP
EVERY-BODY'S MORE RELAXED... HIM TOO.
Ah
THIS IS PROBABLY THE TIME OF DAY HE LOWERS HIS GUARD THE MOST.
FWIP
THERE'S A TIME WHEN HIS FACE TURNS LIGHT PINK...
...IT'S AFTER LUNCH, WHEN WE ALL FEEL A LITTLE SLEEPY.
FWIP

LUB DUB
WE HAVE TO SHOW THEM THEY'RE WRONG.
LUB DUB
WE HAVE TO PROVE TO EVERYONE THAT "WE CAN DO IT IF WE REALLY TRY."

LUB DUB
NA-GISA...
THE STUDENTS IN CLASS E ARE THE LOSERS... THE OUTCASTS...
HE'S GOING TO DO IT!!

LUB DUB
I'D KILL FOR THAT CHANCE!

SWISH
STAB
I HAVE TO GET THEM TO NOTICE ME...
I TOLD YOU AL-READY ...
YOU NEED TO COME UP WITH A BETTER...

...NO MATTER WHAT!
HUG
YOIKS!
...PLAN.
KLNCH
A BB GRENADE!!
THE ASSAS-SINATION SPECIAL!!
GOTCHA!!

KWAA
BOOM

I BET HE WASN'T EXPECTING THAT!!
SUCKS TO BE YOU!!
YEAH! WE DID IT!
ZIP
THAT 10 BILLION IS MINE!!
...STUFFED WITH GUNPOWDER...
...AND THOSE SPECIAL BB'S. MADE QUITE A MESS.
HEY, TERASAKA! WHAT DID YOU GIVE NAGISA?
HUH ?
A TOY GRENADE...
I'LL COVER NAGISA'S MEDICAL BILLS WITH MY 10 BILLION.
DON'T WORRY, IT'S JUST A LITTLE EXPLOSION...
WHAT ...?!

WHAT THE...?
NOT A SCRATCH OR BURN OR ANY-THING...
Uhn...

RIP
IT LOOKS LIKE IT'S PART OF THE OCTOPUS, BUT...
AND WHAT IS THIS FILMY STUFF COVERING NAGISA?

RMBL
RMBL
RMBL
RMBL
RMBL
RMBL
ACTUALLY, I SHED MY SKIN ONCE A MONTH OR SO.
I DON'T LIKE HAVING TO DO THAT.
I COVERED THE BOMB WITH IT TO ABSORB THE EXPLOSION.

...ON HIS FACE...
KRCKL
KRCKL
AND THEN WE SAW A NEW COLOR...

KRCKL
...PITCH BLACK!
KRCKL
HE WAS FURIOUS.
KRCKL

N-NO ...!
WHAT ?
IT WAS NAGISA!
YOU CAME UP WITH THIS PLAN, DIDN'T YOU?!
TERASAKA! YOSHIDA! MURAMATSU!

F
WFF
F
FF
WFF
WFF
WHOSH

SH
OOP

WFF

YOSHIDA
MURAMATSU
TERASAKA
WHAT ...?
HEY ...
YOSHIDA
TERASAKA
TNK
TNK
MURAMATSU
TNK

BUT IF YOU TRY TO ASSASSINATE ME LIKE THAT AGAIN...

THE NAME PLATES... OFF OUR HOUSES?!
I MADE A DEAL...
I PROMISED I WOULD NEVER HARM ANY OF YOU...
DODI
MAEHA
NAKAMURA

...LET ME REMIND YOU THAT EVERYONE ELSE IS FAIR GAME!
HAYAMI
KLTTR
KLTTR
KLTTR
KURAHASHI
KATAOKA
MURA
KEBAYAGI
SUGINO

GR
IN
MAYBE THE WHOLE WORLD... EXCEPT YOU.
YOUR FAMILY... YOUR FRIENDS...
...THERE WAS NO ESCAPE FOR US, NO MATTER WHERE WE WENT.
WE ONLY NEEDED FIVE SECONDS TO REALIZE...
...WAS TO KILL HIM!!
AND THE ONLY WAY TO KEEP EVERYONE SAFE...

YOU'RE A NASTY CREATURE!
WH...
WHAT ARE YOU?!
YOU DISINTEGRATE MOST OF THE MOON AND TELL US YOU'RE GOING TO BLOW UP THE EARTH...
WHY SHOULDN'T WE USE NASTY METHODS TO KILL A NASTY CREATURE?!
NASTY?
I THOUGHT YOUR IDEA WAS WONDERFUL. BRILLIANT.
STRTCH

PAT PAT
ESPECIALLY YOUR CONTRIBUTION, NAGISA.
I GIVE YOU TEN OUT OF TEN FOR YOUR SMOOTH AND NATURAL MOVEMENTS UP UNTIL YOU GRABBED ME.
I WAS TOTALLY CAUGHT OFF-GUARD.
UH-HUH...

HOWEVER ...!
KRCKL
THE REST OF YOU DIDN'T EVEN CONSIDER NAGISA'S SAFETY...
AND NAGISA LET YOU TAKE ADVANTAGE OF HIM!
URK.
YOU'RE BETTER THAN THAT...ALL OF YOU!

I WANT YOU TO ASSASSINATE ME WITH A METHOD THAT BRINGS A SMILE TO YOUR FACE, ONE THAT YOU CAN TAKE PRIDE IN.
YOU'RE MORE THAN CAPABLE OF THAT.
JUST TAKE A FEW WORDS OF ADVICE FROM YOUR TARGET...

HE SCOLDED US AT MACH 20...
THIS CRAZY TENTACLED TEACHER...
...AND PRAISED US.
...THIS WEIRD TEACHER...
...WAS ACTUALLY TAKING A LONG HARD LOOK AT US...
12.25

IF YOU'RE WILLING TO GIVE ME YOUR TIME...
...I'D LIKE YOU TO... TEACH THE CHILDREN FOR ME...
WITH THESE ...
I'M SURE YOU'LL BECOME ...
...A FINE ...
...TEACH-ER...
FSSS
...
WHAT WONDERFUL TENTACLES YOU HAVE!!

WELL THEN... I HAVE A QUESTION FOR YOU, NAGISA...
I HAVE NO INTENTION OF GETTING KILLED.
I'LL ENJOY TEACHING YOU UNTIL THE END OF THE SCHOOL YEAR, AND THEN I'LL DESTROY THE WORLD.
SO WHAT DO YOU NEED TO DO TO PREVENT THAT FROM HAPPENING?
I NEVER THOUGHT OF MYSELF AS AN ASSASSIN BEFORE...
...AND THERE ARE A LOT OF THINGS I HAVE TO LEARN TO BECOME A PROPER ONE...
KLNCH
BUT SOME-HOW I KNOW...

I'LL...
...KILL YOU BEFORE I LET THAT HAPPEN!
...THAT THIS TEACHER...

...WILL BE HAPPY TO SEE ME TRY.
THEN LET'S SEE YOU KILL ME RIGHT NOW.
I'LL LET YOU GO HOME EARLY IF YOU DO!!

AND OUR TARGET IS OUR TEACHER.
Phew.
WE ARE ASSAS-SINS.

...“KORO SENSEI”? IT’S A PUN!
A TEACHER WHO CAN’T BE KILLED...
“KOROSENAI” MEANS “CAN’T BE KILLED.”
“SENSEI” MEANS “TEACHER”...
HOW ABOUT IF WE CALL YOU...
KORO SENSEI AND THE ASSASSINATION CLASSROOM.
IF WE ATTACK HIM NOW, HE’LL POLISH OFF OUR FAMILIES LIKE OUR NAMEPLATES.
I CAN’T GO HOME...
AND THE SCHOOL BELL WILL TOLL AGAIN TOMORROW.

Koro Sensei

- Date of Birth: Unknown
- Height: Around 10 feet if he stretches
- Weight: Lighter than he looks
- Career History: Agent of destruction/ Teacher of Class E
- Hobby/Skill: Supersonic speed cruising
- Motto: Education and Assassination in One!
- Weakness: Unknown
- Strong Point: Easy to draw

This criminal element destroyed our moon.
And vows to destroy the earth in a year's time.
Beware of his numerous extraordinary abilities.
ten billion dollar award for him, dead not alive.

THE AMERICAN NEWSPAPERS ARE FULL OF ARTICLES ABOUT THE MOON'S DESTRUCTION AS WELL...
SLUURP
The K.Y. Times
Moon Havoc Continues...
I WISH THEY'D PUT SOMETHING MORE INTERESTING ON THEIR FRONT PAGE.

...WITH AN AMERICAN NEWSPAPER AND A FRESH DRINK HE PICKED UP IN HAWAII AT MACH 20.
EVERY MORNING BEFORE HOMEROOM, HE KICKS BACK AND RELAXES BEHIND THE SCHOOL BUILDING...

OH YEAH!
THAT COOL 10 BILLION IS MINE!!
GRIP
GOOD LUCK, SUGINO!
SURE.
IT'S JUST LIKE YOU TOLD ME.
THANKS, NAGISA.

WE ARE...
STRTCH
...ASSAS-SINS.
AND OUR TARGET IS...
WHO
...OUR TEACHER.
OOSH

COME NOW...
YOU SHOULD ALWAYS REPLY WHEN SOMEONE GREETS YOU.

GOOD MORNING...
...NAGISA, SUGINO...

RSSTL
...
GOOD MORNING, KORO SENSEI!
HUH?!
WHA—?!

I LIKE YOUR IDEA OF COVERING THE BALL IN ANTI-"ME" BB'S.
BUT UNLIKE AN AIR GUN, IT DOESN'T MAKE A SOUND WHEN THROWN.
FSSSSS

Slow Motion Replay
BUT...
I HAD SOME TIME BEFORE THE BALL REACHED ME...
FWA
ZZIP
AND SINCE I CAN'T TOUCH THOSE BB'S WITHOUT HURTING MYSELF...
KREEK
THNK
ZO
OSH
Courage
KREEK
Courage
Courage
RSTL
RSTL

WHAT THE ...?!
I WENT OVER...
...TO THE STOREROOM TO GET A BASEBALL GLOVE.
I REALLY DO HOPE YOU MANAGE TO KILL ME...
...BEFORE GRADUA-TION.
TIME FOR HOMEROOM.
OKAY.
SURE ...

OUR MISSION...
...IS TO KILL OUR TEACHER.
IF WE SUCCEED, WE GET 10 BILLION DOLLARS!

HEY, NAGISA!
I HEARD SUGINO BLEW IT WHEN HE TRIED TO ASSASSINATE KORO SENSEI THIS MORNING!
UH-HUH.

DON'T KNOW WHY...
IT'S NOT LIKE ANYONE ELSE HAS DONE IT.

HE'S BEEN DEPRESSED EVER SINCE.

KORO SENSEI...
OUR INVULNER-ABLE TEACHER.

IT'S IMPOSSIBLE, MR. KARASUMA.
HE'S TOO FAST.

HAVE YOU FIGURED OUT A WAY TO KILL HIM YET?
RE-PORT!
Ministry of Defense
Special Projects Dept.
Tadaomi Karasuma

HOW ARE WE SUPPOSED TO KILL A GUY WHO CAN FLY AT MACH 20?!
HE'S GONNA DROP BY NEW YORK CITY TO CATCH A BASEBALL GAME.
YOU KNOW WHAT HE'S DOING TODAY AFTER SCHOOL?
WOOO
OOSH

AFTER ALL, HE ALWAYS RETURNS EVERY WEEKDAY TO TEACH YOU.

...WHERE THE ARMIES OF THE WORLD CANNOT.
I HAVE FAITH THAT YOU'LL SUCCEED...

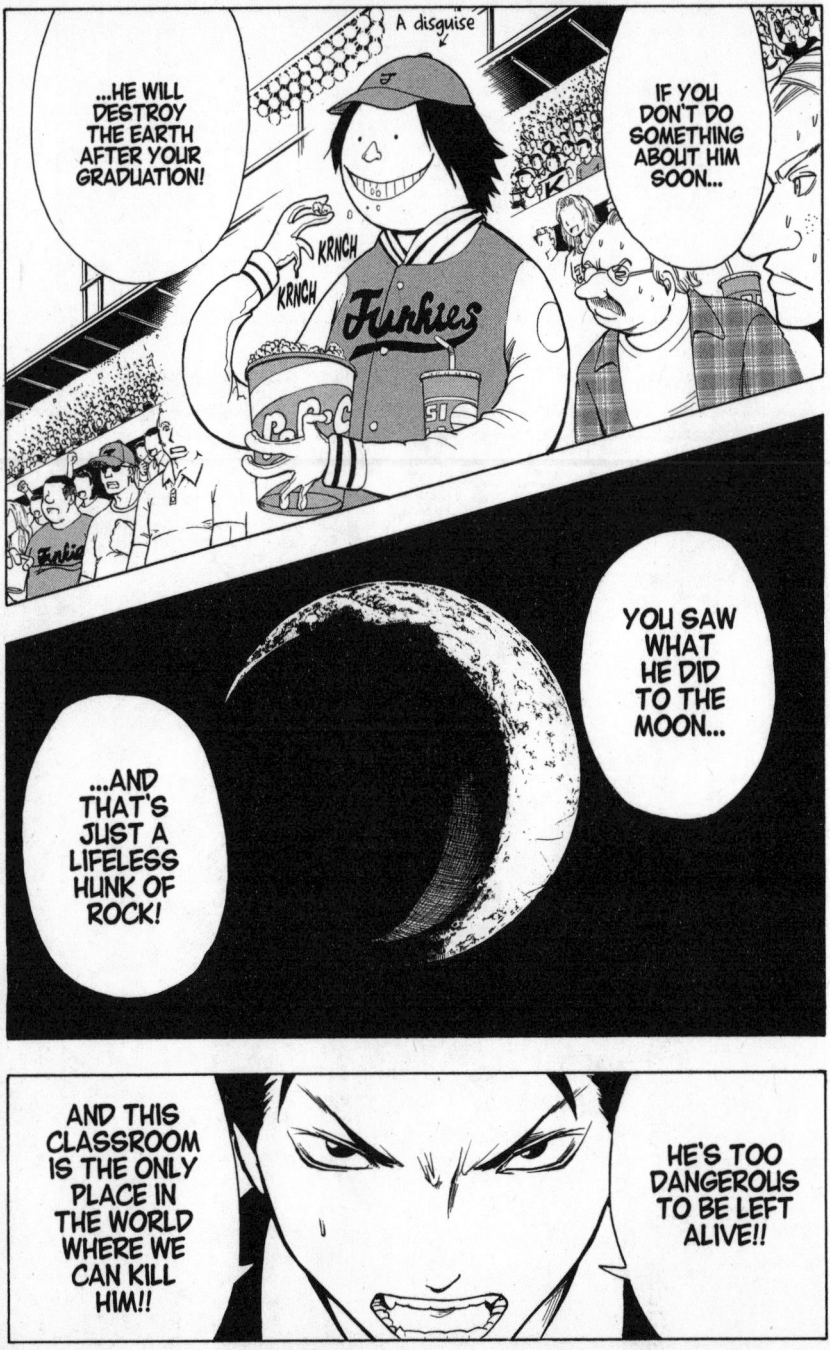
A disguise
...HE WILL DESTROY THE EARTH AFTER YOUR GRADUATION!
IF YOU DON'T DO SOMETHING ABOUT HIM SOON...
KRNCH
KRNCH
Funkies
YOU SAW WHAT HE DID TO THE MOON...
...AND THAT'S JUST A LIFELESS HUNK OF ROCK!
AND THIS CLASSROOM IS THE ONLY PLACE IN THE WORLD WHERE WE CAN KILL HIM!!
HE'S TOO DANGEROUS TO BE LEFT ALIVE!!

THE STUDENTS OF CLASS E, THE CLASS OF LOSERS AND REJECTS...
...HAVE BEEN GIVEN AN OPPORTUNITY TO SAVE THE WORLD AND BECOME HEROES.
BUT WE DON'T EVEN KNOW WHY...
...KORO SENSEI WANTS TO DESTROY THE WORLD.
OR WHY...
...HE BECAME OUR TEACHER.
RING RING RING RING

KRNCH KRNCH
WHAT ARE YOU EATING?
KORO SENSEI...?
WANT A BITE?
A COCONUT I BOUGHT IN HAWAII.
PEOPLE USUALLY DRINK THE JUICE, YOU KNOW...
I POLISHED IT AND GOT THE SCUFF MARKS OFF IT, SUGINO.
PHNK
Sigh...
THE WAY YOU MOVE I'D NEVER HAVE BEEN ABLE TO HIT YOU IN THE FIRST PLACE.
YEAH, RIGHT.
THAT WAS A NICE PITCH YESTERDAY WHEN YOU TRIED TO ASSASSINATE ME.
I USED TO BE.
TOSS
USED TO BE?
ARE YOU ON THE BASEBALL TEAM?

IF YOU END UP IN CLASS E...
...YOU DON'T GET TO DO SPORTS OR ANY EXTRA-CURRICULAR ACTIVITIES ANYMORE.

SINCE WE'RE HERE BECAUSE OF OUR BAD GRADES...
...WE'RE SUPPOSED TO FOCUS ON STUDYING.
YOU PROBABLY THINK THAT'S UNFAIR.

WHAT-EVER.
I DON'T CARE ANYMORE.

YOU SAW ME PITCH YESTER-DAY...
MY PITCHES SUCK.
THEY'RE TOO SLOW.

AND HERE I AM IN CLASS E!
FIGURES. I SUCK AT BASEBALL... I SUCK AT SCHOOL...
"JUNK PITCHES." OTHER TEAMS COULDN'T MISS 'EM...
...SO I GOT SCRATCHED FROM THE STARTING LINEUP.
LET ME GIVE YOU SOME ADVICE.
SUGINO ...
I HOPE HE ISN'T PICKING ON HIM...
...BECAUSE OF HIS ASSAS-SINATION ATTEMPT YESTERDAY.
POP
I HAVE TO TURN IN THIS ASSIGNMENT BEFORE CLASS.
I THINK HE'S TALKING TO SUGINO.
FWIP-FWIP

OH NO! IT'S WORSE THAN I THOUGHT!

WHAT HAPPENED TO "NOT HARMING THE STUDENTS" ?!
WHAT ARE YOU DOING TO HIM?!
RSTL RSTL

GLURGH!
SUGINO ...
...YOUR PITCHING FORM...
YOU MODELED IT AFTER ARITA, DIDN'T YOU? THE PITCHER WHO WENT TO THE MAJORS IN NEW YORK...
THE MUSCLES IN YOUR SHOULDER AREN'T AS DEFINED AS HIS.
EVEN IF YOU COPIED HIM EXACTLY, YOU'D NEVER BE ABLE TO THROW A FASTBALL LIKE HE DOES.
MY TENTA-CLES...
...KNOW ALL AND SEE ALL. META-PHORICALLY SPEAKING.
PHUMP
H-HOW ...
...CAN YOU BE SO SURE ABOUT THAT?

I CHECKED HIM OUT YESTERDAY. MY TENTACLES KNOW ALL AND SEE ALL.
TENTACLES ATTA
From Underground
Pitcher Arita all tangled up!

GREAT ...
I KNEW IT.
I'VE GOT NOTHING.
I WOULDN'T SAY THAT.

AND LOOK ...
Damn you, Tentacles!!
Arita
AND HE SIGNED ONE FOR YOU?!
AFTER THAT YOU ASKED HIM FOR HIS AUTO-GRAPH?!

HIS TENTACLES REALLY DO KNOW ALL!

THE FLEXIBILITY OF YOUR ELBOW AND WRIST IS REMARKABLE.
IF YOU LEARN HOW TO USE THAT TO YOUR ADVANTAGE, EVENTUALLY YOU'LL BE BETTER THAN ARITA!
TRUST ME...MY TENTACLES DON'T LIE.
FLOOP
THERE ISN'T JUST ONE WAY TO HAVE TALENT.
YOU JUST NEED TO FIND A METHOD THAT SUITS YOUR SKILL SET.

SPLORCH
SPLORCH

MY...
...
"TALENT"
...

MY ELBOW AND WRIST...
...ARE BETTER THAN HIS...

!!

OF COURSE.
I'M HIS TEACHER.
NEW YORK ...
YOU WENT ALL THE WAY THERE FOR SUGINO?
FWIP

KORO SENSEI!

COME TO THINK OF IT, OTHER TEACHERS WOULDN'T DESTROY THE WORLD EITHER...
OTHER TEACHERS WOULDN'T DO THAT...

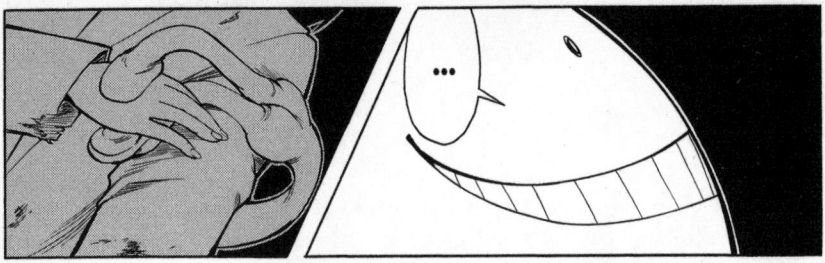
...

NAGISA...
I BECAME YOUR TEACHER BECAUSE I MADE A PROMISE TO SOMEONE...

OH, I'LL STILL DESTROY THE EARTH...
...BUT I'M YOUR TEACHER FIRST AND FOREMOST.
WSSH
WSSH
WSSH
WSSH

AND TO HELP YOU CONFRONT YOUR PROBLEMS HEAD-ON...
...MIGHT BE MORE IMPORTANT THAN DESTROYING THE EARTH.
Great!!!
96
April 23
My favorite food
Yesterday, I went to a Sushi Shop with my family to celebrate the birthday on my father. Sushi is the most favorite food of my father, and of course me! Therefore, a lot of all motive ingredients in the menu of the Sushi Shop, but my most favorite ingredient is octopus. Its tuna and texture is so wonderful that I enjoying ordered it yesterday. And when I ate it, my teacher appeared in my mind because his tentacle looks like the octopus. I wonder the taste of my teacher's tentacle...
That's right!
I love sushi too!!
My favorite ingredient is botan-ebi.
No major mistakes in your grammar and you even end the last sentence with a joke. This is a wonderful diary entry!!
—Koro-Sensei
Celebrate
This should be plural!

HUH ?!
IT'S GREAT GETTING OUR ASSIGNMENTS BACK SO QUICKLY...
I THOUGHT YOU'D LIKE THEM...
BUT WHAT'S WITH THE WEIRD EXTRA CREDIT QUESTIONS?
Bonus! ♡
Write a one-page essay explaining why this tentacle is just downright adorable.
IT'S MORE LIKE A PUNISH-MENT!

...
KORO SENSEI...

OR...
MNCH
MNCH
...SOMETHING LIKE THAT. YOU'LL NEVER KILL ME, BUT MAYBE THAT DOESN'T MATTER.

WELL ...
I WANT YOU TO FIND JOY—AS A STUDENT AND A WOULD-BE ASSASSIN.
SPZZZ

OUR TEACHER...

OUR TARGET...
TO TELL THE TRUTH, I REALLY DON'T THINK WE CAN KILL HIM.

I'M WORKING ON A BREAKING BALL THAT MAKES FULL USE OF MY ELBOW AND WRIST.
THIS AND A CHANGE-UP MAKE FOR A GOOD ARSENAL.

SMASH
WHOA!

HEH...
THAT WAS AMAZING, SUGINO!!
IT LOOKED LIKE THE BALL DISAP-PEARED!!

...ON BASE-BALL...
...AND ASSAS-SINATION.
NAGISA ...
I REFUSE TO GIVE UP...

IT'S STILL IMPOSSIBLY SLOW FOR KORO SENSEI THOUGH...

SOME-HOW...
...HE MANAGES TO MOTIVATE US.
YEAH.
I WANT TO KILL YOU, SO COULD YOU PLEASE COME OUTSIDE AND PLAY CATCH?
KORO SENSEI!
HA HA HA! YOU DON'T GIVE UP, DO YOU?
YOU LEARN MORE THAN YOU THINK IN KORO SENSEI'S ASSASSINATION CLASSROOM!
Nagasaki-Pork-Belly Bun

E-11 NAGISA SHIOTA

- BIRTHDAY: JULY 20
- HEIGHT: 5' 3"
- WEIGHT: 106 LBS.
- FAVORITE SUBJECT: ENGLISH
- LEAST FAVORITE SUBJECT: SCIENCE
- HOBBY/SKILL: RESEARCH!
- FUTURE GOAL: NONE
- PERSONALITY TYPE: HERBIVORE
- IF HE GETS THE 10 BILLION: FIND A WAY TO GROW TALLER

C'MON!
WE'LL SHARE THE 10 BILLION!!
HE'S MAKING SNOW CONES FOR SNACK TIME.
YEAH... USING ICE HE JUST GOT FROM THE NORTH POLE.
GRNCH GRNCH
THERE HE IS!
CLASS 3 THE PERFECT TIME TO HELP OUT

CAN I HAVE A SNOW CONE?
FWIP
FWIP
KORO SENSEI!!

SNIFF
LOOK AT THOSE BIG GRINS...
THE STUDENTS ARE FINALLY GETTING IT!

Me too! Me too!
Koro Sensei!
AWW...

SHNK
SHNK
CLASS 3
THE PERFECT TIME TO HELP OUT
AND THEY'RE ALL TRYING TO KILL ME!

SWIP
JUST SO YOU KNOW...
SWIP
SWIP

PLNK
NOW GET RID OF THOSE DANGEROUS ANTI-"ME" KNIVES...
PLNK

YOUR SMILES LOOKED A BIT FORCED.
NOT CONVINCING ENOUGH TO GET ME TO LET MY GUARD DOWN.

HEY!

LOOK !!
...AND PUT A...
...GENUINE SMILE ON YOUR FACE BY... APPRECIATING THE BEAUTY OF THESE FLOWERS!
HUH ?
HOW COULD YOU, KORO SENSEI?
I'M SOR-RY... I DIDN'T KNOW ...
WE'VE BEEN GROWING THEM FOR WEEKS...
I'LL GO GET...
THOSE ARE OUR FLOWERS!!
KORO SENSEI !!
UM... THEY ARE ?!
HUH ?!
... SOME NEW BULBS FOR YOU.
WHAMP
WHAMP

HANDLE EACH BULB WITH CARE!
RIGHT...
YOU CAN'T PLANT FLOWERS AT MACH 20!
DIG
DIG
OF COURSE...
...BUT I GUESS THAT DOESN'T INCLUDE TULIPS.
I THOUGHT SO...
...DOESN'T HE WANT TO DESTROY THE WORLD?
HEY...

HE'S ONLY TRYING TO MAKE HIMSELF LOOK GOOD.
PFFT...

IT MIGHT HELP US ASSASSINATE HIM SOMEDAY.
SORTA. I'M WRITING DOWN KORO SENSEI'S WEAKNESSES.
HM...

WHAT ARE YOU DOING? HOMEWORK?
NAGISA...

WE ARE...
...ASSAS-SINS.
Koro Sensei's Weakness #1
He messes up when he shows off
...
SO...
...ANY IDEA HOW?
AND THIS IS THE ASSASSINATION CLASSROOM, CLASS 3-E.
AND ...
Principal's Office
TOMORROW I TAKE OVER AS THEIR P.E. TEACHER.
YOU'VE PROBABLY ALREADY BEEN INFORMED BY THE MINISTRY OF DEFENSE.

I TRUST YOU.
BUT THE STUDENTS' EDUCATION AND SAFETY IS MY TOP PRIORITY.
Principa
AND PROVIDE TECHNICAL AND MORAL SUPPORT FOR THE STUDENTS.
I CAN KEEP AN EYE ON HIM.
DON'T WORRY... I HAVE A TEACHING CREDENTIAL.
KUNUGIGAOKA JUNIOR HIGH... WHERE THE BEST OF THE BEST GO...
...AND THE WORST OF THE WORST GO TO CLASS 3-E.

A MONSTER WITH ENOUGH POWER TO DESTROY THE EARTH...
THE MILITARY IS USELESS AGAINST HIM... BUT FOR SOME REASON HE WANTS TO BE A TEACHER!

PLEASE ...
HE'S BEING PAID A PRETTY PENNY TO LET US IN HERE.
THE PRINCIPAL WAS VERY UNDER-STANDING.

OF COURSE HE'S UNDER-STANDING.

JUST THE KIDS IN CLASS 3-E. NO ONE ELSE CAN FIND OUT.

THE ONLY ONES WHO KNOW ABOUT THIS...
...ARE US, THE PRINCIPAL AND CLASS 3-E.

SERI-OUSLY ?!
THAT SUCKS... IF YOU GO THERE YOU'RE DONE FOR.
CRAP!
THEY'LL KICK ME INTO CLASS E IF MY GRADES GET ANY WORSE.
THE OTHER STUDENTS AND TEACHERS TREAT THE 3-E STUDENTS LIKE GARBAGE!
THE ANNEX IS HORRIBLE. NO CAFETERIA... DIRTY BATHROOMS...
AND UNLESS YOU BELIEVE IN MIRACLES... YOU'LL NEVER LEAVE.
YEAH ...
I'VE GOTTA STUDY HARDER SO I DON'T END UP IN 3-E!
I'D RATHER DIE THAN GET SENT THERE!
TALK ABOUT THE END CLASS...

I SEE...
...BY TREATING CLASS 3-E SO POORLY...
...THE OTHER "NORMAL" STUDENTS WORK HARDER TO FEEL SUPERIOR TO THEM—AND OUT OF FEAR OF WINDING UP THERE.

BUT IT MUST BE HELLISH...
...FOR THE BOTTOM-OF-THE-HEAP STUDENTS IN THAT CLASS!

HARSH, BUT EFFECTIVE.
THIS SYSTEM GIVES US THE PERFECT SETTING FOR AN ASSAS-SINATION...

OH, MR. KARASUMA!
HELLO!!
HELLO.

KRNCH
KRNCH

UH...NO. BY THE WAY... WHERE IS HE?
WELL...

TMP
I'LL BE TAKING OVER AS YOUR P.E. TEACHER STARTING TOMORROW.
REALLY?!
I HOPE WE GET ALONG.
DOES THAT MEAN WE HAVE TO CALL YOU "COACH"?
TMP

OKAY!
I BROUGHT THE POLES AND ROPES!
...AND HE WANTS TO MAKE UP FOR IT, SO...
KORO SENSEI RUINED OUR FLOWERBED...

ZLIP
ZLIP
...HE'S LETTING US PLAY "PIÑATA."
GET HIM!!
PA
SWISH
POW
SWISH
WE STILL CAN'T HIT HIM?!
DAMN IT!

YOU NEED TO TRY HARDER.
I'M ONLY GOING TO LET YOU DO THIS ONCE.
STAB
STAB

BUT YOU KNOW ...
OBSERVING HIS WEAK-NESSES...
TCH...
IS THIS EVEN AN ASSAS-SINATION ATTEMPT?!
YEAH ...
HE'S JUST MESSING WITH US.
WHAT DO YOU THINK, NA-GISA?

KRCK
KRCK
YOU'D THINK SOMEONE WOULD BE ABLE TO—

HA HA HA! WHAT'S WRONG WITH YOU, CLASS E?
IT DOESN'T GET ANY EASIER THAN THIS!

OH.
SN
AP

FWUMP

KILL HIM, NOW!!
EEP EEP
TMP TMP
Koro Sensei's Weakness #1
He messes up when he shows off.
AAAHH !!
LET'S SEE WHAT ELSE...
YEAH ...
HUH ...
YOUR NOTES MIGHT COME IN HANDY.
THE ROPE'S TANGLED IN MY TENTA-CLES!
TIME OUT!
STAB
WAIT...
SWIFF
TIME OUT!
Koro Sensei's Weakness #2
Panics easily.

KADUNK
WO
CRAP!
OOSH
DAMN IT, HE GOT AWAY!!
HUMPH ...
AND WE WERE SO CLOSE!
TOLD YOU I WAS BETTER THAN YOU, NYAAAH NYAAAH!
BET YOU CAN'T CATCH ME UP HERE!
THAT'S SO UNFAIR !!!!
JUST FOR THAT... DOUBLE THE HOMEWORK!
Koro Sensei's Weakness #3
Sore loser
Phew...
HFF HFF HFF

JUNIOR HIGH SCHOOL STUDENTS CHEERFULLY DISCUSSING MURDER...
IF IT WEREN'T NECESSARY, IT WOULD BE CREEPY.
BUT THIS WAS OUR BEST ATTEMPT YET!
FOOOSH
HE'S RUN-NING AWAY ...
WHAT SHOULD I DO WITH THE 10 BILLION I GET FOR KILLING HIM?
OOOH...
IF WE KEEP THIS UP, I KNOW WE'LL KILL HIM SOONER OR LATER!!
WHAT DO YOU THINK?
CAN WE KILL KORO SENSEI?
NA-GISA ...

WE JUST HAVE TO GO ALL OUT.
WE'LL KILL HIM.
FUNNY THING IS...
...OUT OF ALL THE KIDS AT THIS SCHOOL...
...THE ONES IN CLASS E ARE THE MOST OPTIMISTIC.
ZOOOP

IF YOU DO, WE WILL BE FORCED TO ERASE YOUR MEMORY.
FREAKY ...!

THAT'S EVERY-THING...
TO PREVENT A PANIC, YOU ARE FORBIDDEN FROM SPEAKING ABOUT THIS.

THE OTHER STUDENTS IN CLASS E HAVE ALREADY BEEN BRIEFED...
...AND ARE ALREADY WORKING ON THEIR MISSION.

ONCE YOUR SUSPENSION IS OVER...
...
...WE ASSUME YOU WILL DO THE SAME.

IT'S HARMLESS TO HUMANS BUT HIGHLY EFFECTIVE AGAINST THE TARGET.
IT CAN.
CAN THIS RUBBER KNIFE REALLY HURT HIM?
HEY...
BOING
BOING
SH
COOL. HUMAN OR NOT...
HM...
UNK
WANTED
...HOW LONG I'VE BEEN ITCHING TO KILL A TEACHER...
...YOU HAVE NO IDEA...

School Policies for the Kunugigaoka Junior High Special Placement Class.

For students who have been transferred to the Special Placement Class (Class 3-E) due to poor academic performance.

- All classes will be held in building 3-E. At no time will students be allowed to enter the main school building without special permission.
- To avoid distraction from their studies, students are forbidden to take part in extracurricular activities.
- All other classes receive priority consideration for special activities over Class 3-E.
- If students put in the effort and earn good grades in 3-E, they will be allowed to return to their previous class.
- Students who are still in 3-E at the end of the second trimester will not be permitted to graduate.
- Students transferred into 3-E must abide by the above school policies and are hereby advised that they will be strictly enforced.

Kunugigaoka School Mascot

Kunudon

CLASS 4 TIME TO GET DOWN TO WORK

SWISH

Five, six, seven, eight...

Three, four...

One, two...

SWISH

SWISH

AND KEEP YOUR BALANCE!!

AGAIN, FROM ATTACK STANCE ONE!!

IF ONLY THEY WEREN'T WIELDING WEAPONS...

LEAVE US ALONE. GO PLAY IN THE SANDBOX OR SOMETHING.
YOU'RE NOT LISTENING, ARE YOU?

I'M THE NEW P.E. TEACHER.
I THOUGHT I TOLD YOU TO TAKE A BREAK.
Why are you wearing that?

THE STUDENTS *LOVED* MY P.E. CLASS!
WHY ARE YOU SO MEAN, MR. KARASUMA?
NOT REALLY...

I'LL DEMON-STRATE HOW IT'S DONE FIRST.
OKAY, THIS IS *REALLY* SIMPLE...

LIKE THE OTHER DAY...
...YOUR SIDE-STEPPING EXERCISE ...

Koro Sensei
Koro Sensei
Koro Sensei

VISUAL CLONING?!
ONCE YOU GET THE HANG OF THAT, WE'LL ADD IN CAT'S CRADLE.
WE'LL START WITH HIGH-SPEED VISUAL CLONING.

WHA——...?!
YEAH, BUT I WANT TO LEARN P.E. FOR HUMAN BODIES!
IT WAS PRETTY COOL...

WHY ARE WE DOING THIS, MR. KARASUMA ?
ESPECIALLY WITH OUR TARGET RIGHT IN FRONT OF US...WATCHING OUR EVERY MOVE.

FINALLY SOME PEACE AND QUIET.
LET'S GET ON WITH THE CLASS.
Sniff!
Sniff!
ro Sensei

THE BETTER YOU KNOW THE BASICS, THE BETTER YOU'LL PERFORM.
ASSASSINATION IS A SKILL LIKE ANY OTHER.

TRY AND HIT ME WITH THAT RUBBER KNIFE.
FOR EXAMPLE... LET'S SEE...
MAE-HARA!
ISOGAI!

HMM ...

LIM...
LIH...
TMP

JAB
OKAY!

WHAT ...?
ARE YOU SURE?
IT WON'T HURT HUMANS.
IF YOU HIT ME, I'LL LET CLASS OUT EARLY.
THE TWO OF US? AT THE SAME TIME?

JI
NK

HAI-YA!

THAT IT?
AHH...

WIFF
BA
WFF
F
WIFF
SEE WHAT YOU CAN DO...
WIFF
BAMP
SWISH
...WITH A LITTLE TRAINING?
SMAK
DAMN!
WOW...

YA
NK
FLIP
WHOA!
ACK!
...HOW ARE YOU GOING TO HIT SOMEONE WHO CAN MOVE AT MACH 20?
IF YOU CAN'T HIT ME...

GRIN
HE CHANGED HIS OUTFIT, MADE GREEN TEA, AND BUILT A SAND CASTLE...
SHOW-OFF...
HUMM...
WE MUST HAVE BORED HIM.

...YOU'LL BETTER YOUR CHANCES OF HITTING HIM.
IF YOU CAN IMPROVE YOUR SKILLS ENOUGH TO HIT ME...
HMPF

YOU'RE GOING TO LEARN THEM ALL IN MY CLASS!
KNIVES, PISTOLS, SNIPER RIFLES, ASSAULT WEAPONS... THE BASICS OF ASSASSINATION...
RING
RING
RING
RING

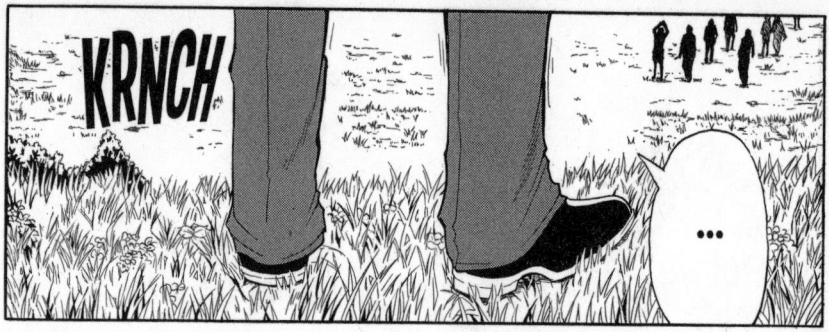
KRNCH
...

"THE SCHOOL DISTRICT MAY ADD EXTRA TEACH-ERS..."
"...TO PROVIDE ASSISTANCE AT ANY TIME IF THE NEED ARISES."
IF I REMEMBER YOUR CONTRACT CORRECTLY...

MR. KARASUMA'S KINDA SCARY...BUT HE'S COOL.
YEAH!
I THINK I'M GOING TO ENJOY P.E. FROM NOW ON.

MR. KARA-SUMA...
YOU'RE TRYING TO WIN THEM OVER, AREN'T YOU?
WHAT KIND OF A JOKE IS THIS?
SKWEEK
RSTL

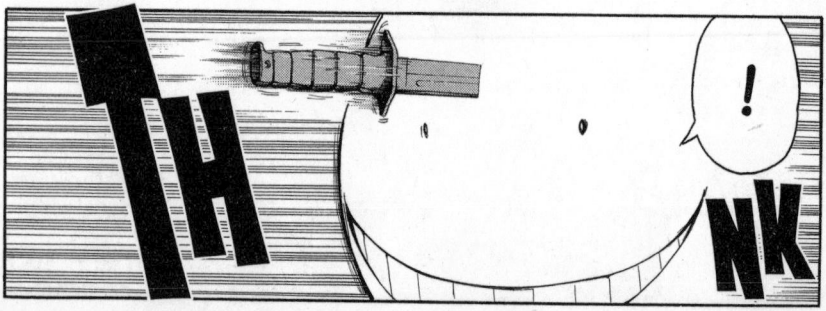
!
TH
NK

MY JOB IS TO OVERSEE THESE ASSASSINS...
TINK
...UNTIL THEY ASSAS-SINATE YOU.
THE STUDENTS GAVE IT TO ME. PLEASE CALL ME "KORO SENSEI."
GRIN
I HAVE A NAME...
HUH?
WE HAVE A TEST AFTER THIS...
LOOK WHO'S HERE...
WSSH
IT WOULD BE AWE-SOME IF P.E. WAS OUR LAST CLASS FOR THE DAY!

WSSH
WSSH
HIYA.
LONG TIME NO SEE, NAGISA.
YOU'RE BACK!
KARMA ...

FWIP
HE LOOKS LIKE AN OCTOPUS. FREAKY.
WHOA!
SO THAT'S KORO SENSEI?

FWIP
HMM...
FWIP

HEH HEH ...
I GOT USED TO SLEEPING IN.
BEING LATE ON YOUR FIRST DAY BACK FROM SUSPEN-SION DOESN'T LOOK GOOD.

YOU WERE SUPPOSED TO COME TO CLASS THIS MORNING.
KARMA AKABANE...?

I LOOK FORWARD TO A PRODUCTIVE YEAR TOGETHER.
NICE TO MEET YOU TOO.
GRP

IT'S NICE TO MEET YOU, KORO SENSEI!!
KIDDING! SORRY I'M LATE.

FSs
SSS
!
SNKT
SHIF
SHIF

YOINK

FSSSS

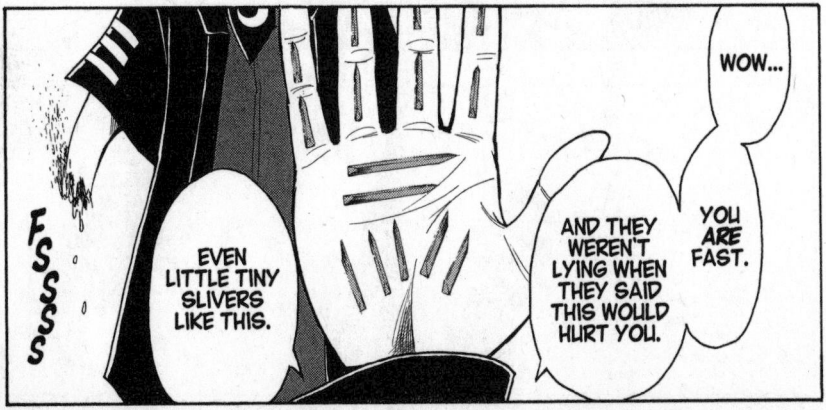
WOW...
YOU ARE FAST.
AND THEY WEREN'T LYING WHEN THEY SAID THIS WOULD HURT YOU.
EVEN LITTLE TINY SLIVERS LIKE THIS.
FSSSS

AND LOOK AT YOU WAY OVER THERE. YOU SCARED? BWAK BWAK BWAK...
TMP
I CAN'T BELIEVE...
...YOU FELL FOR THE OLDEST TRICK IN THE BOOK!

TMP
TMP
SCHLORP
...ANYONE HAS INFLICTED DAMAGE ON KORO SENSEI!!
THIS IS THE FIRST TIME...

TMP
!
"KORO SENSEI..." THAT'S A PLAY ON "KORO SENAI" ISN'T IT...? "CAN'T KILL"...

YOU KNOW...
...I THINK THEY GOT YOUR NAME WRONG.
TWTCH
TWTCH
TWTCH
TWTCH

ORDINARY TEACHERS COULDN'T HANDLE HIM. I GUESS THEY FINALLY SENT HIM TO 3-E.
BUT HE KEPT GETTING SUSPENDED FOR FIGHTING.

NA-GISA...
I HAVEN'T BEEN IN CLASS E THAT LONG, SO... WHO'S THAT GUY?
WHAT'S HIS STORY?

WELL ...
WE WERE IN THE SAME CLASS MY FIRST AND SECOND YEAR...

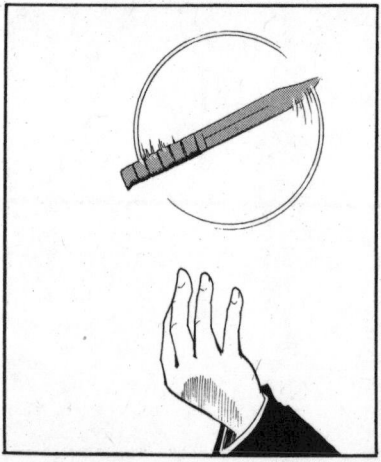

BUT KNOWING KARMA ...
...HE'LL BE AT THE HEAD OF THE CLASS IN NO TIME.
HUH ?
WHAT DO YOU MEAN?
KICK

...KARMA IS PROBABLY THE BEST OUT OF ALL OF US.
WHEN IT COMES TO WEAPONRY, BATTLE TACTICS, AND SNEAK ATTACKS...

TING
TING
DON'T RUN TOO FAR, KORO SENSEI.
TING
I DON'T NEED THE EXERCISE...I JUST NEED TO KILL YOU.

TADAOMI KARASUMA

- BIRTHDAY: AUGUST 15 (28 YEARS OLD)
- HEIGHT: 5' 11"
- WEIGHT: 187 LBS.
- CAREER HISTORY: 1ST AIRBORNE BRIGADE→ INTER-SERVICES INTELLIGENCE → CONTINGENCY SPECIAL PROJECTS DEPARTMENT→ CLASS 3-E PE TEACHER.
- HOBBY/SKILLS: GENERAL COMBAT
- MOTTO: DO THE POSSIBLE AND CARRY OUT THE IMPOSSIBLE.
- FAVORITE ANIMAL: DOG
- DOGS: THEY BARK LIKE CRAZY WHEN HE PASSES.

CLASS 5 MAKING TIME FOR KARMA

HE'S MAD BECAUSE KARMA GOT THE BETTER OF HIM.

AH...

BOING

MAYBE HE'S PUNCHING THE WALL?

BOING

IF THAT'S AS HARD AS HE CAN HIT THAT'S PRETTY SAD.

BOING

Koro Sensei's Weakness #4

Weak punches.

TERASAKA KNOWS ALL ABOUT MAKING HIM MAD.
HEY, KARMA...
YOU DON'T WANT TO GET THAT MONSTER MAD, YOU KNOW.
HEH.
DIDJA WET YOUR PANTS AFTER YOU PISSED HIM OFF?
HEY, TERA-SAKA ...
OF COURSE I MADE HIM MAD. I ALMOST KILLED HIM...
QUIET DURING THE TEST!!
HEY, YOU TWO!!
TELL IT TO YOUR TENTA-CLES!
TSK TSK
WHA ...?
SLAM
I DID NOT!! THAT'S ...
YOU WANNA PIECE OF ME?!

!!
YOU KNOW YOU'RE NOT ALLOWED TO EAT IN CLASS.
WHERE DID YOU GET THAT, ANYWAY?
SORRY, KORO SENSEI.
I'M DONE WITH MY TEST NOW.
SO I'LL JUST SIT HERE AND EAT MY GELATO.
OOPS. MY BAD.
I FOUND IT IN THE FREEZER IN THE FACULTY ROOM.
I HAD TO FLY THROUGH THE STRATOSPHERE TO KEEP IT FROM MELTING ON MY WAY BACK!! AND THE STRATOSPHERE IS COLD!!
"MY BAD"?!
IT'S YOURS?!
THAT'S MY GELATO!! I BOUGHT IT IN ITALY YESTERDAY !!
HEY! THAT...

FLOOP
"SQUISHY-PUNCH"?
...
NO. I'M JUST GOING TO EAT WHAT'S LEFT OF MY GELATO!!

SO WHAT ARE YOU GONNA DO ABOUT IT?
HM...
SQUISHY-PUNCH ME?

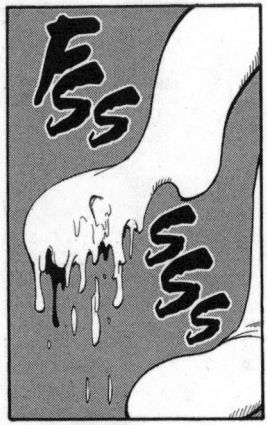
FSS
SSS

!!
FS
SS

WHAT?
WHEN DID HE PUT THOSE ON THE FLOOR?!
SKTTL
ANTI-ME BB'S...

HA HA!
YOU FELL FOR IT AGAIN.
PAPOW
PAPOW
!
PAPOW
I'M GOING TO KEEP THIS UP, YOU KNOW.
YOU THINK I CARE IF I DISRUPT YOUR CLASS?
SKRTCH
IF YOU DON'T LIKE IT...
...KILL MY PARENTS... KILL WHOEVER...
...

I'VE BEEN WANTING...
...TO KILL A TEACHER.
BUT ONCE YOU DO...
...YOU WON'T BE A TEACHER ANYMORE...
...YOU'LL BE A MONSTER.
SPLO
RCH

HERE'S MY TEST.
I KNOW I ACED IT.
!

SEE YOU, KORO SENSEI...
SHFF
LET'S PLAY AGAIN TOMORROW!

...
...AND HE'S TRYING TO PUSH KORO SENSEI RIGHT TO THAT EDGE.

KARMA IS REALLY SMART...

LIKE RIGHT NOW...
HE KNOWS THERE'S A LINE KORO SENSEI CAN'T CROSS...

THE SAD THING IS...
...HE DOES THAT WITH EVERY-BODY—
FWIP
FWIP
...PUSHES THEM RIGHT TO THE EDGE...
HE DOESN'T TRUST ANYONE.

HMPH...
THANKS TO HIM, I HAVE TO GO GET A NEW GELATO.
WEEEZZZZZZZZZ
Test: History
Karma Akabane
HE'S SMART. AND HE'S RIGHT...
I CAN'T KILL OR HARM HIM...
...IF I WANT TO KEEP WORKING AS A TEACHER.
SO...
...WHAT SHOULD I DO WITH HIM...?

Kunugigaoka Station
BYE, NAGISA!
BYE!
SEE YOU TOMOR-ROW!

FREAK FITS RIGHT INTO 3-E.
OF COURSE... HE'S A LOSER.
I DON'T THINK HE'S EVER COMING BACK TO OUR CLASS.

HEY...
IT'S NAGISA.

GUESS WHAT!
I HEARD AKABANE GOT SENT THERE AFTER HIS SUSPENSION.
WHOA! THAT SUCKS!
I'D RATHER DIE THAN END UP IN 3-E!

YOU'D RATHER DIE?
REALLY?
SHATTR
THEN HOW ABOUT RIGHT NOW?

KAR-MA...
HA HA HA... THEY SERIOUSLY THOUGHT I WAS GONNA KILL THEM.

AKABANE!!
DASH
AAAH!!

I DON'T HAVE TIME TO GET SUSPENDED AGAIN...
...NOW THAT I HAVE A NEW TOY TO PLAY WITH...

YOU KNOW A LOT ABOUT KORO SENSEI, RIGHT?
UM... I GUESS...
A LITTLE BIT...
SO, NA-GISA...
...THERE'S SOMETHING I'VE BEEN MEANING TO ASK YOU.

WOULD HE GET MAD...
...IF I CALLED HIM AN OCTOPUS?
AN... OCTO-PUS...?
HMM. PROB-ABLY NOT...
HE MIGHT EVEN TAKE IT AS A COMPLI-MENT.

SHUF SHUF
AND THE OTHER DAY, HE DUG A HOLE IN THE SCHOOL-YARD AND...

HE SIGNS HIS TESTS WITH AN OCTOPUS.
AND HE USES AN OCTOPUS AVATAR WHEN HE PLAYS VIDEO GAMES...
sodium
Octopus X!!
A lot of students make this mistake. Be careful!!

HELP! I'M STUCK IN AN OCTOPUS POT!
HE MADE AN OCTOPUS JOKE?!
THE OCTOPUS IS BECOMING HIS TRADEMARK.
It was funny, though.
YEAH YEAH ...
HMM...
I JUST GOT THIS CRAZY IDEA...
GRIN
急行 通過します。
KARMA ...
WHAT ARE YOU UP TO...?

RM MMM
I CAN'T BELIEVE I GET TO KILL A TEACHER WITH MY OWN HANDS!
IT'S PAYBACK TIME! AFTER WHAT HAPPENED WITH THE LAST ONE...
MMM
HNNNK HNNNK
I AM...
...REALLY HAPPY. REALLY HAPPY.
I WAS AFRAID HE WAS GOING TO TURN OUT TO BE JUST SOME WEIRD MONSTER ...
...BUT HE ACTUALLY IS A TEACHER. A REAL TEACHER.
...?

CAN MY DAY GET ANY WORSE?
I DIDN'T HAVE ENOUGH MONEY TO BUY A GELATO.
AND I WON'T GET ANY MORE TILL PAYDAY.
GUESS I'M EATING IN TONIGHT.
THERE ARE SOME COOKING UTENSILS IN THE STOREROOM I CAN USE...
GOOD MORNING.
...
LIM...
WHAT'S THE MATTER, EVERYONE?
SHFF

I AM SO SORRY.
I THOUGHT IT WAS YOU...AND I KILLED IT.
I'LL THROW IT AWAY FOR YOU, IF YOU HAND IT TO ME.
...?
OKAY.
SPLORCH

I'LL START OFF BY...
I DON'T NEED TO KILL YOU JUST YET...
COME ON, KORO SENSEI...
...MAKING YOU WISH YOU WERE DEAD!
FZZ ZZ
WHA ...?!

WOOSH
WSSSPF
LET ME SHOW YOU SOMETHING, KARMA...
VROOOOOSH
THE SPEED OF MY DRILL TENTACLES...
AND THE FIREPOWER OF THE MISSILE I TOOK FROM THE NAVY.

FZZZ
ZZZZ
ZZZZ
ZZZ
ZZZP
PPP
SWISH
I WILL NEVER ...
...LET AN ASSASSIN GET AWAY SCOT-FREE.

YOU LOOK PALE. YOU SKIPPED BREAKFAST, DIDN'T YOU?
AACK ...

!!

...

OCTOPUS DUMPLINGS COOKED AT MACH 20!
IT'S THE MOST IMPORTANT MEAL OF THE DAY! BREAKFAST, THAT IS.
WFF WFF
WFF WFF

KARMA, IT IS MY JOB...
...TO POLISH YOU...
...AN ASSASSIN'S BLADE THAT HAS BECOME RUSTY AND DULL.

COME AT ME WITH EVERYTHING YOU'VE GOT ALL DAY LONG.
AND I'LL KEEP POLISHING YOU...
!!
...BY THE END OF CLASS TODAY...
...YOUR BODY AND SPIRIT WILL BE SPARKLY CLEAN.

Never cut corners.

That is the secret to harassment.

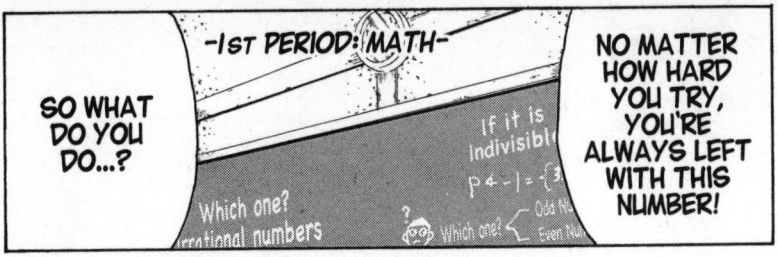

CLASS 6 | IT'S TIME TO MAKE A CHOICE

CLASS 6
IT'S TIME TO MAKE A CHOICE
...ADD THESE ALL UP TOGETHER...
NOW ...
AND THEN... TO OUR SURPRISE...
TA-DAH!
KLNCH
KLNCH
KLNCH
KLNCH
YOUR ANSWER!
WAY TOO SLOW, KARMA.
be divided by 36.
Solved.
I MEAN, REALLY...
I HAD ENOUGH TIME TO DO YOUR NAILS TOO. YOU LIKE THEM?
!!

-4TH PERIOD: HOME ECONOMICS-
HAS YOUR GROUP FINISHED, FUWA?
HMM, I DON'T KNOW...
I KNOW ...
WHY DON'T YOU MAKE IT AGAIN?
LET ME TRY IT.
IT'S TOO BITTER...
AH!
GET RID OF THIS BATCH FIRST.
SMAK

WHAT THE-?!
AND DON'T WORRY ABOUT THE SOUP.
I GOT IT ALL WITH AN EYEDROPPER.
ZUP ZUP ZUP ZUP ZUP ZUP
ALWAYS WEAR AN APRON IN THE KITCHEN, KARMA.
I EVEN ADDED A PINCH OF SUGAR.
HEY...
...IT'S PERFECT NOW!!
SNKR
Ha ha...

-5TH PERIOD: LITERATURE-

EXCERPT FROM KENSAKU SHIMAKI'S "THE RED FROG."

WOOOSH
NIBBL NIBBL
KAR-MA...
THERE'S NO RUSH. WE'LL KILL HIM TOGETHER... EVENTUALLY.
ONCE KORO SENSEI'S ON TO YOU...
...IT'S IMPOSSIBLE TO KILL HIM BY YOURSELF, NO MATTER WHAT YOU DO.
HE'S NO ORDINARY TEACHER, AFTER ALL.
TEACHER, HUH...
...

BUT AS LONG AS YOU DO WHAT'S RIGHT...
...I'LL BACK YOU UP!!
IT HAS THE POTENTIAL TO GET YOU INTO A LOT OF TROUBLE...
YOUR ATTITUDE... NEEDS WORK...
AKABANE !!
I DON'T WANT HIM DROPPING DEAD ANYWHERE ELSE.
I WANNA KILL HIM MYSELF.
HELL NO...
FLOOP
KARMA...
I SURE DID A LOT OF WORK ON YOUR HAIR TODAY.
SURE ...

CAN I ASK YOU SOME-THING?
YOU'RE A TEACHER, RIGHT, KORO SENSEI?
YES.
I AM.
...I HAVE PLENTY MORE HAIRSPRAY AND NAIL POLISH.
BUT IF YOU WANT TO KEEP ON TRYING TO KILL ME...
HEH.
WOOSH
...PROTECT THEIR STUDENTS— WITH THEIR LIVES, YEAH?
AND TEACH-ERS...
OF COURSE.
THAT'S WHAT TEACHERS DO.
KLCK
THAT'S GOOD TO HEAR.
THEN I'VE GOT YOU...

...TEACH!
JUMP
COME HELP ME AND...
...I'LL SHOOT AND KILL YOU.

...YOU'RE DEAD AS A TEACHER.
LET ME FALL TO MY DOOM AND...
YOUR LIFE REALLY DOES FLASH BEFORE YOUR EYES...
FREAKY...
3-E
3-E... AS IN THAT CLASS?
YOU OKAY?
HUH?
OF COURSE I WAS IN THE RIGHT.
THEY PICKED ON YOU BECAUSE OF SOMETHING STUPID LIKE THAT?
WHAT COULD POSSIBLY BE WRONG WITH PROTECTING A STUDENT FROM A BULLY?

WHAT ?!
YOU WERE CLEARLY IN THE WRONG.
NO, AKABÁNE.
HUH ?
WAIT A MINUTE...
YOU BEAT UP THE SCHOOL VALEDIC-TORIAN! YOU CAN'T DO THAT!
ARE YOU NUTS?!
AND WHO'S GOING TO BE HELD RESPONSIBLE IF THIS SCREWS UP HIS HIGH SCHOOL PLACEMENT EXAMS? ME!
Jeez...
YOU BEAT UP A STUDENT WITH A FUTURE—A BRIGHT FUTURE—JUST BECAUSE HE PICKED ON A STUDENT IN CLASS E!! CLASS E.
YOU TOLD ME YOU HAD MY BACK...
YOU SAID YOU'D ALWAYS BE ON MY SIDE...

IT'S LIKE HE'S DYING INSIDE...

ZZPPPPPPFFFF
KA
FLWU
MP
WHAT ...?!

I TAKE MY HAT OFF TO YOU FOR THIS BRILLIANTLY STRATEGIZED ASSASSINATION ATTEMPT.
KARMA...

SPLITCH
SO...
...I DECIDED TO BECOME A LITTLE STICKY.
IT'S ANYTHING GOES WITH THOSE TENTACLES !!
DAMN IT...

BUT IF I SAVED YOU SLOWLY, YOU'D SHOOT ME.
IF I SAVED YOU AT SUPERSONIC SPEED, YOUR BODY COULDN'T HANDLE IT.
POP

OH, AND BY THE WAY...
ACK...
NOW YOU CAN'T SHOOT ME! AHAHAHA-HAHAHA...

THIS IS HOPELESS.

HE WON'T DIE AND I CAN'T KILL HIM...

...NOT AS A TEACHER ...
AT LEAST...
IT WAS THE BEST PLAN I HAD YET...
OKAY... MAYBE NOT THE BEST...
KARMA ...
I CAN'T BELIEVE YOU DID THAT!
WELL ...
OUT OF IDEAS AL-READY ?
THAT'S A SHAME...
OOH, LOOK AT ALL THE PRODUCT I HAVEN'T HAD A CHANCE TO USE ON YOU YET...
I GUESS YOU'RE ACTUALLY MORE OF A SLACKER THAN I THOUGHT.

SLICE
...TOMORROW OR SO...
I'LL KILL YOU...
...
I STILL WANT TO KILL HIM.
Hmph
BUT ...
I FEEL DIFFERENT ABOUT IT NOW.
DOESN'T NEED AS MUCH POLISHING UP.
HE'S READY FOR CLEAN AND HEALTHY ASSAS-SINATIONS NOW.
GRIN

LET'S GO HOME, NAGISA.
WE CAN GET A BITE TO EAT ON THE WAY.
HEY!
THAT'S MY WALLET !!
YEAH? WELL, YOU...
...SHOULDN'T LEAVE IT LYING AROUND THE FACULTY ROOM.
GIVE IT BACK !!
SURE.
BUT IT'S EMPTY!!
ANY ASSASSIN WHO TRIES TO KILL KORO SENSEI...
...GETS SPARKLING CLEAN— MORE THAN THEY BARGAINED FOR.
IT WAS JUST NICKELS AND DIMES. I THREW THEM IN A DONATION BOX.
WHAT?! YOU, YOU... ROBIN HOOD!!
THAT'S THE ASSASSINATION CLASSROOM FOR YOU.
HEY, HOW SHOULD WE KILL HIM TOMORROW...?

Assassination Will Keep Us Together

I'LL TAKE THESE, THANK YOU....
...AND THAT'S HOW YOU GET THE ARTIFICIAL COLOR OUT OF SNACKS...
RING
RING
RING
RING

WAIT... WHY IS HE DRAWING A SALARY IF HE'S PLANNING TO DESTROY THE WORLD...?
HE JUST DOESN'T WANT TO WAIT TILL PAYDAY TO GET SNACKS.
Hey! We bought those!
COOKIES

LUB DUB
LUB DUB
CLASS 7 TIME FOR A REFRESHING DRINK

FWIP
COOKIES

KORO SEN-SEI...
UM...
YEAH... UM...

Class 7 Time for a Refreshing Drink

IT'S POISON!!

PLEASE DRINK IT!!

FWUMP

OKUDA...
WHAT KIND OF IDIOT WOULD DRINK THAT AFTER YOU—
I'M NOT GOOD AT SURPRISE ATTACKS LIKE EVERYONE ELSE...
BUT...
...I LOVE CHEMISTRY! AND I REALLY PUT MY HEART AND SOUL INTO THIS...
WOW!
TRMBL
TRMBL
THIS IS...
THIS...
TRMBL
LEMME TRY IT!
IS THAT SO?
GULP
HE DRANK IT!!

PLOINK

HE GREW HORNS!
...SODIUM HYDROXIDE.
HARMFUL TO HUMANS BUT NOT TO ME.
OH ...

Umnh.
URRGH.
GYURGH...

YOU'VE GOT TWO MORE.
I'LL GIVE THEM A TRY TOO.
UM ...
YES ...!

FLAP

AND THE LAST ONE...
THALLIUM ACETATE.
ACTUALLY LOOKS KINDA COOL.
NOW HE GREW WINGS!!

HOW WILL HE TRANSFORM THIS TIME?!
LUB DUB
LUB DUB
WHATTYA THINK WILL HAPPEN NOW?!
LUB DUB

UMM...
TALK ABOUT EXPRESSION-LESS!!
AQUA REGIA...
THAT'S ALL THEY DID TO ME, HUH?
UHH...

"DON'T HATE ME BECAUSE I'M BEAUTI-FUL."
WHAT'S HE TALKING ABOUT?!

YOU LOOK LIKE AN EMOTICON !!
HE DOES!

RIGHT...
I APOLOGIZE...
NOW, OKUDA...
...YOU KNOW I CAN'T ALLOW A STUDENT TO CONCOCT DANGEROUS POISONS WITHOUT SUPERVISION.
OKAY!
UM...
DO YOU HAVE TIME AFTER SCHOOL TODAY?
WE CAN RESEARCH A POISON THAT CAN KILL ME—TOGETHER!
I DON'T SEE THAT ENDING WELL...
YEAH...
SHE'S GOING TO...
...MAKE POISON... WITH THE POISON'S TARGET?

NOW ADD THE ETHANOL TO IT.
AND BE CAREFUL NOT TO BREATHE IN THE FUMES.
OKAY!
YOUR GRADES IN CHEMISTRY ARE EXCELLENT, BUT...
I GET TERRIBLE GRADES IN EVERYTHING ELSE.
YEAH, I KNOW...
IT'S NO WONDER I WAS TRANSFERRED TO CLASS E.
ESPECIALLY IN...
...WRITING.
I JUST CAN'T...
...FIND THE RIGHT WORDS TO SAY WHAT I FEEL!
I NEVER KNOW WHAT THE RIGHT ANSWER IS!
BUT... WITH MATH AND SCIENCE...
...THERE'S IS A RIGHT ANSWER.
...

RIGHT...
SCRBBL SCRBBL
SO I...
...OR TO THINK ABOUT COMPLI-CATED EMOTIONS...
...DON'T NEED BEAUTIFUL WORDS...
BUT I HAVE...
...A LITTLE HOMEWORK FOR YOU.
BAM
Step (1)
NH4Cl
35%
+
Na2S2
THIS IS...
...THE POISON HE ASKED YOU TO MAKE?
IT IS!!
HE SAID THIS POISON WOULD BE MOST EFFECTIVE!!

I THINK HE REALLY GETS ME.
IT'S EASIER TO UNDERSTAND AS A MANGA. I CAN FOCUS ON MY STRENGTHS.
HE EVEN DREW A MANGA ABOUT HOW TO STORE IT PROPERLY.
THAT'S OUR KORO SENSEI... ALWAYS TRYING TO HELP.
Storing It Wrong
Storing It Right!
KORO SENSEI! HERE...!
OH.
THERE HE IS. WHY DON'T YOU GIVE IT TO HIM?
SHFF
I CAN'T WAIT!
WELL DONE...
I'LL TAKE IT RIGHT AWAY.
GULP
GULP
GULP

OKUDA...
AHA HAHA HAHA HA...
LUB
DUB
UM...
WHAT DO YOU MEAN...?
SHA
TTR
LUB DUB
...THANKS TO YOUR POTION...
...I CAN MOVE ON TO THE NEXT LEVEL.
LUB DUB
LUB DUB
G
Y
U
U
U
U
U
R
G
H!
TI
NG
!!

Phew.

HE MELTED!!

SPLORP
TNK

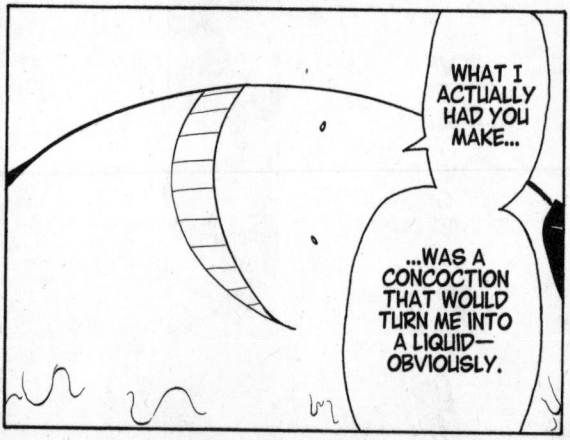
WHAT I ACTUALLY HAD YOU MAKE...
...WAS A CONCOCTION THAT WOULD TURN ME INTO A LIQUID—OBVIOUSLY.

...I CAN LEAK THROUGH THE SMALLEST OF SPACES!!
AND NOW THAT I'M A LIQUID...
LET'S SEE IF YOU CAN KILL ME NOW!!
TO TOP IT OFF, I'M STILL AS FAST AS BEFORE!!
SWOOSH
PING PING
PING
PING PING
SPLORCH
SWISH
WZZZ
I NEVER KILLED A LIQUID METAL SLIME IN THAT GAME EITHER...
HEY...
IT WAS HARD ENOUGH BEFORE!!
THERE'S NO WAY WE CAN HIT YOU WHEN YOU KEEP HIDING IN THE CEILING AND UNDERNEATH THE FLOOR-BOARDS!!
FWIP
FWIP
FWIP
FWIP
FWIP

La la la
SO YOU...
...LIED TO ME, KORO SENSEI?!
KORO SENSEI TOLD YOU THAT WAS POISON?
OKUDA...
UM ...
OKUDA ...
YOU NEED GOOD COMMUNICATION SKILLS TO DECEIVE PEOPLE IF YOU'RE TO HAVE ANY HOPE OF ASSASSINATING THEM.
Poison
Poison
NO MATTER HOW GOOD YOU ARE AT CREATING POISONS...
...YOUR TARGET IS ONLY GOING TO USE THEM AGAINST YOU.
...IF YOU JUST HAND THEM OVER...
Poison
WHAT...?

NA-GISA...
HOW WOULD YOU POISON ME?
ME?
HMM...
I'D PROBABLY MIX THE POISON INTO YOUR JUICE...
...AND OFFER IT TO YOU SAYING IT WAS A SPECIAL HOMEMADE DRINK I MADE...
...I GUESS.
EX-ACTLY.
IN ORDER TO DECEIVE SOMEONE, YOU NEED TO UNDERSTAND HOW THEY FEEL, WHAT MOTIVATES THEM.
YOU NEED TO INTERPRET... COMMUNI-CATE...
THE SKILLS YOU DEVELOP THROUGH READING AND WRITING...
...ARE NECESSARY FOR A GOOD POISONING.

YES...
YOUR CHEMISTRY SKILLS WILL COME IN HANDY IN THE FUTURE.
The effect wore off.
BUT YOU'LL NEED TO WORK ON YOUR COMMUNICATION SKILLS...
...BECAUSE ONE WAY OR ANOTHER... YOU'RE GOING TO HAVE TO EXPLAIN YOUR WORK SO THAT OTHERS CAN UNDERSTAND IT.
SCHLORP
I UNDERSTAND.
HEH HEH ...
THIS ISN'T JUST ABOUT ASSASSINATION.

EVEN A MASTER CHEMIST...
...TURNS INTO AN ORDINARY STUDENT BEFORE KORO SENSEI.
WE'RE STILL ...
...FAR FROM BEING THE SKILLED ASSASSINS WHO CAN KILL KORO SENSEI.

I SEE ...
BUT DON'T YOU THINK...
...THAT MIGHT FRIGHTEN THE STUDENTS?

WE DON'T BELIEVE THOSE CHILDREN ARE CAPABLE OF KILLING HIM.
THIS IS AN ORDER!
WHAT'S WORSE? FRIGHTENING THE STUDENTS? OR PANICKING THE ENTIRE WORLD?
KARASUMA...
BUT...
SO...
...WHAT IS THIS... OPERATIVE... LIKE?
VERY SKILLED...
ELEVEN CONFIRMED AROUND THE WORLD.

WE'RE SENDING IN...
...A REAL PROFESSIONAL.
LICK
TO BE CONTINUED...

RECESS: KORO SENSEI'S DRAWING SONG

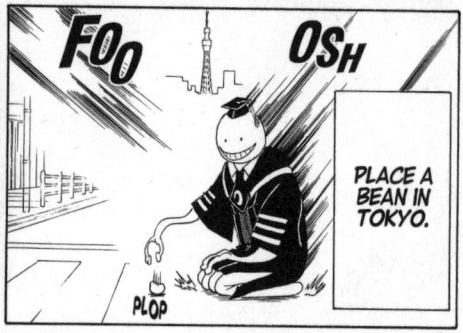

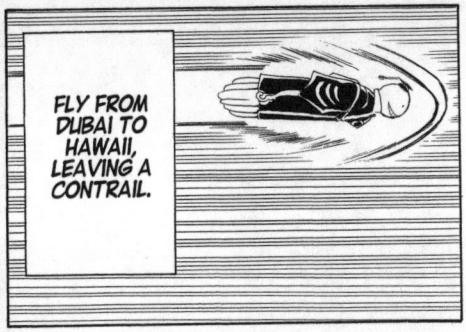
FLY FROM DUBAI TO HAWAII, LEAVING A CONTRAIL.

NOW BACK TO DUBAI FROM HAWAII VIA THE PHILIPPINES.

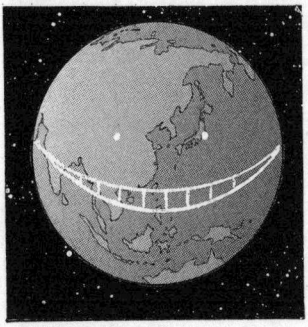

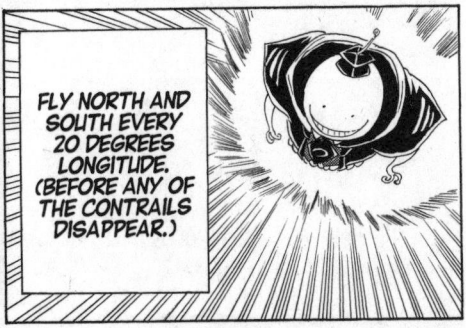
FLY NORTH AND SOUTH EVERY 20 DEGREES LONGITUDE. (BEFORE ANY OF THE CONTRAILS DISAPPEAR.)

LIKE HELL WE CAN DRAW THAT!!
YOUR TURN!
OKAY ...
AND THERE YOU HAVE IT! A KORO SENSEI!
~Recess (End)

"Kill" is a fascinating word. It's often used, but rarely put into action.

So I decided to create a story centered around this unique word.

If you enjoy it, you can kill me now and I'll die happy.

—Yusei Matsui

Yusei Matsui was born on the last day of January in Saitama Prefecture, Japan. He has been drawing manga since elementary school. Some of his favorite manga series are *Bobobo-bo Bo-bobo*, *JoJo's Bizarre Adventure* and *Ultimate Muscle*. Matsui learned his trade working as an assistant to manga artist Yoshio Sawai, creator of *Bobobo-bo Bo-bobo*. In 2005, Matsui debuted his original manga *Neuro: Supernatural Detective* in *Weekly Shonen Jump*. In 2007, *Neuro* was adapted into an anime. In 2012, *Assassination Classroom* began serialization in *Weekly Shonen Jump*.

Yellow is his usual face color. Koro Sensei often changes the color of his face, but this is the one you'll see most often.

ASSASSINATION CLASSROOM

YUSEI MATSUI

1

TIME FOR ASSASSINATION

A MOMENT OF TENTACLE ZEN

I have no idea what kind of weapon will be used in World War III. But World War IV will be fought with tentacles.

—Koro Sensei

ASSASSINATION CLASSROOM

Volume 1
SHONEN JUMP ADVANCED Manga Edition

Story and Art by YUSEI MATSUI

Translation/Tetsuichiro Miyaki
English Adaptation/Bryant Turnage
Touch-up Art & Lettering/Stephen Dutro
Cover & Interior Design/Sam Elzway
Editor/Annette Roman

ANSATSU KYOSHITSU © 2012 by Yusei Matsui
All rights reserved.
First published in Japan in 2012 by SHUEISHA Inc., Tokyo.
English translation rights arranged by SHUEISHA Inc.

The stories, characters and incidents mentioned in this publication are entirely fictional.

No portion of this book may be reproduced or transmitted in any form or by any means without written permission from the copyright holders.

Printed in the U.S.A.

Published by VIZ Media, LLC
P.O. Box 77010
San Francisco, CA 94107

10 9 8 7
First printing, December 2014
Seventh printing, September 2017

www.viz.com
www.shonenjump.com

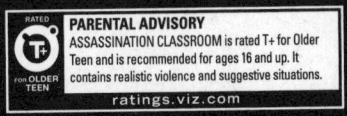

Syllabus for Assassination Classroom, Vol. 2

A sexy new teacher comes to Class 3-E to do the students' job for them. When the 3-E students begin exhibiting signs of self-esteem, Principal Asano demands that Koro Sensei crush their spirits so they continue to set a bad example for the rest of the school to rise above. But Koro Sensei has other plans... Then a class field trip goes terribly wrong after two 3-E girls are abducted. Who will come to their rescue...?

Available NOW!

MY HERO ACADEMIA

IZUKU MIDORIYA WANTS TO BE A HERO MORE THAN ANYTHING, BUT HE HASN'T GOT AN OUNCE OF POWER IN HIM. WITH NO CHANCE OF GETTING INTO THE U.A. HIGH SCHOOL FOR HEROES, HIS LIFE IS LOOKING LIKE A DEAD END. THEN AN ENCOUNTER WITH ALL MIGHT, THE GREATEST HERO OF ALL, GIVES HIM A CHANCE TO CHANGE HIS DESTINY...

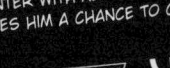

viz media

www.viz.com

BOKU NO HERO ACADEMIA © 2014 by Kohei Horikoshi/SHUEISHA Inc.

SHOYO HINATA IS OUT TO PROVE THAT IN VOLLEYBALL YOU DON'T NEED TO BE TALL TO FLY!

HAIKYU!!

Story and Art by HARUICHI FURUDATE

Ever since he saw the legendary player known as the "Little Giant" compete at the national volleyball finals, Shoyo Hinata has been aiming to be the best volleyball player ever! He decides to join the team at the high school the Little Giant went to—and then surpass him. Who says you need to be tall to play volleyball when you can jump higher than anyone else?

viz media

You're Reading in the Wrong Direction!!

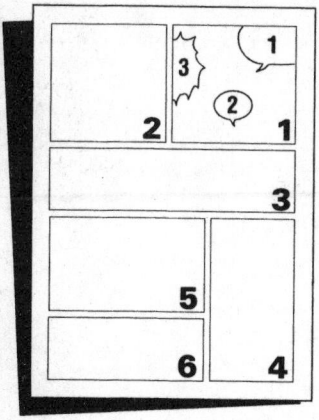

Whoops! Guess what? You're starting at the wrong end of the comic!

...It's true! In keeping with the original Japanese format, **Assassination Classroom** is meant to be read from right to left, starting in the upper-right corner.

Unlike English, which is read from left to right, Japanese is read from right to left, meaning that action, sound effects and word-balloon order are completely reversed... something which can make readers unfamiliar with Japanese feel pretty backwards themselves. For this reason, manga or Japanese comics published in the U.S. in English have sometimes been published "flopped"—that is, printed in exact reverse order, as though seen from the other side of a mirror.

By flopping pages, U.S. publishers can avoid confusing readers, but the compromise is not without its downside. For one thing, a character in a flopped manga series who once wore in the original Japanese version a T-shirt emblazoned with "M A Y" (as in "the merry month of") now wears one which reads "Y A M"! Additionally, many manga creators in Japan are themselves unhappy with the process, as some feel the mirror-imaging of their art skews their original intentions.

We are proud to bring you Yusei Matsui's **Assassination Classroom** in the original unflopped format.
For now, though, turn to the other side of the book and let the adventure begin...!

—Editor

THE ACTION-PACKED SUPERHERO COMEDY ABOUT ONE MAN'S AMBITION TO BE A HERO FOR FUN!

ONE-PUNCH MAN

STORY BY ONE | ART BY YUSUKE MURATA

Nothing about Saitama passes the eyeball test when it comes to superheroes, from his lifeless expression to his bald head to his unimpressive physique. However, this average-looking guy has a not-so-average problem—he just can't seem to find an opponent strong enough to take on!

Can he finally find an opponent who can go toe-to-toe with him and give his life some meaning? Or is he doomed to a life of superpowered boredom?

viz media
www.viz.com

ONE-PUNCH MAN © 2012 by ONE, Yusuke Murata/SHUEISHA Inc.